ECLIPSED

ECLIPSED

DANAI GURIRA

THEATRE COMMUNICATIONS GROUP
NEW YORK
2016

Eclipsed is published by Theatre Communications Group, Inc., 520 Eighth Avenue, 24th Floor, New York, NY 10018-4156

This volume is published in arrangement with Oberon Books Ltd, 521 Caledonian Road, London, N7 9RH.

This publication is made possible in part by the New York State Council on the Arts with the support of Governor Andrew Cuomo and the New York State Legislature.

TCG books are exclusively distributed to the book trade by Consortium Book Sales and Distribution.

A catalogue record for this book is available from the Library of Congress.

ISBN 978-1-55936-527-7 (paperback)
ISBN 978-1-55936-853-7 (ebook)

Cover design by Scott McKowen
Front cover photo by David Cooper
Back cover photo by Rafael Navarro

First TCG Edition, September 2015
Revised TCG Edition, January 2017
Second Printing, December 2018

To the courageous women of Liberia and of every war zone.

To my Auntie Dora, your light will never dim in our hearts.

The world premiere of *Eclipsed* was produced by Woolly Mammoth Theatre Company (Howard Shalwitz, Artistic Director; Jeffrey Herrmann, Managing Director) in Washington, D.C., on August 31, 2009. The play was directed by Liesl Tommy. The scenic design was by Daniel Ettinger, the lighting design was by Colin K. Bills, the costume design was by Kathleen Geldard, the sound design was by Veronika Vorel; the production stage manager was Rebecca Berlin. The cast was:

THE GIRL	Ayesha Ngaujah
HELENA	Uzo Aduba
BESSIE	Liz Femi Wilson
MAIMA	Jessica Frances Dukes
RITA	Dawn Ursula

Eclipsed was produced by Center Theatre Group (Michael Ritchie, Artistic Director; Charles Dillingham, Managing Director) in Los Angeles, on September 13, 2009. The play was directed by Robert O'Hara. The scenic design was by Sibyl Wickersheimer, the lighting design was by Christopher Kuhl, the costume design was by Alex Jaeger, the sound design was by Adam Phalen, the original music was by Kathryn Bostic; the production stage manager was Amy Bristol Brownewell. The cast was:

THE GIRL	Miriam F. Glover
HELENA	Bahni Turpin
BESSIE	Edwina Findley
MAIMA	Kelly M. Jenrette
RITA	Michael Hyatt

Eclipsed was produced by Yale Repertory Theatre (James Bundy, Artistic Director; Victoria Nolan, Managing Director) in New Haven, Connecticut, on October 23, 2009. The play was directed by Liesl Tommy. The scenic design was by Germán Cardenás, the lighting design was by Marcus Doshi, the costume design was by Elizabeth Barrett Groth, the sound design and original music was by Broken Chord Collective; the dramaturg was Walter Byongsok Chon and the production stage manager was Karen Hashley. The cast was:

THE GIRL	Adepero Oduye
HELENA	Stacey Sargeant
BESSIE	Pascale Armand
MAIMA	Zainab Jah
RITA	Shona Tucker

Eclipsed had its New York premiere at The Public Theater (Oskar Eustis, Artistic Director; Patrick Willingham, Executive Director) on October 14, 2015. The play was directed by Liesl Tommy. The scenic and costume design was by Clint Ramos, the lighting design was by Jennifer Schriever, the sound design and original music was by Broken Chord Collective; the production stage manager was Diane DiVita. The cast was:

THE GIRL	Lupita Nyong'o
HELENA	Saycon Sengbloh
BESSIE	Pascale Armand
MAIMA	Zainab Jah
RITA	Akosua Busia

Eclipsed was developed with the support of McCarter Theatre Center (Emily Mann, Artistic Director) and developed by the Ojai Playwrights Conference (Robert Egan, Artistic Director).

Eclipsed opened on Broadway at the Golden Theatre on March 6, 2016. The producers were Stephen C. Byrd, Alia Jones-Harvey, Paula Marie Black, Carole Shorenstein Hays, Alani Lala Anthony, Michael Magers, Kenny Ozoude, Willette Klausner, Davelle, Dominion Pictures, Emanon Productions, FG Productions, The Forstalls and MA Theatricals. The artistic team and cast remained the same as The Public Theater production.

CHARACTERS

THE GIRL, fifteen

HELENA, late teens/early twenties

BESSIE, mid-late teens

MAIMA, mid-late teens

RITA, forties

SETTING

Liberia: Bomi County, a LURD rebel army
camp, 2003

ACT ONE

SCENE ONE

LURD Rebel Army Camp Base. HELENA and BESSIE, 'wives' of a Commanding Officer, sit. It is a dilapidated shelter; it may once have been someone's decent home. It is riddled with bullet holes and black soot and mortar residue, it is a partially indoor enclosure. Piles of used ammunition litter one corner. The enclosure is well organized, however, with obvious areas for cooking, sleeping and bathing. A tattered Liberian flag hangs on the back wall.

Lights up on HELENA sitting on a metal tub, styling BESSIE's wig. BESSIE is six and a half months pregnant. They look offstage.

HELENA: *(Getting up.)* Does dat look like the CO to you?

BESSIE: Sorry! I tought I smell him, he has dis smell, I can smell it, can't you smell it? Maybe it just me who know his smell well well. Let's leave ha for few minute.

(HELENA pushes her over and lets THE GIRL out from under the tub.)

BESSIE: *(To THE GIRL.)* Sorry.

(Pulls her wig off, goes and sits down next to tub again.)

BESSIE: Can you finish? *(Indicating hair.)* It making my wig not sit right.

HELENA: Come. *(Starts to finish braiding BESSIE's hair.)*

(To THE GIRL). So den whot happen when he go back?

THE GIRL: Oh, ya, dere dis one joke I no tell you, one time de servant call him, he say, he say, 'You sweat from a baboon's balls.' *(Laughing.)*

(HELENA and BESSIE are quiet.)

HELENA: Whot dat?

THE GIRL: It baboon sweating in de, de man parts – den he calling him dat.

9

HELENA: Oh…ahh…ahh ha, ya dat funny, dat funny.

BESSIE: So in de end he stay wit de African wife?

THE GIRL: Wait! He lovin de American gal so she say no den he go back to Zamunda in Africa

HELENA: Where Zamunda – I neva hear of no Zamunda

THE GIRL: It not real.

HELENA: Oh.

BESSIE: Why he no be from Liberia?

THE GIRL: I don't know. So he come back and dey have a big, big weddin.

BESSIE: Wit de African gal!

THE GIRL: WAIT! So we all tinking it wit de African gal and she walking wit de big wedding dress.

BESSIE: African wedding dress?

THE GIRL: Ahhh…no…it woz de white one

BESSIE: Oh…dose ones borin.

THE GIRL: Ya. So he looking sad sad cause he tink it gon be de African one – and den, and den she get to de front and it NOT! It de American gal!

BESSIE: So…de American gal win.

THE GIRL: NO!! Dat de woman he love.

HELENA: But he could have been wit me or you or ha – but de American tek him. And you say he Prince wit lot o money. He could have been wit poor African gal, den she can hep ha family. You say ha fada have restaurant – so she no need dat hep. I no like dat.

THE GIRL: NO! It movie – it not real, it just a story.

HELENA: I no like dat story. I goin –

(HELENA jumps and puts tub roughly over THE GIRL, and sits on it, BESSIE resumes her position. Both look up at a man and watch him, they jump into line as though in an army formation. BESSIE responds to him, gestures at herself, puts on her wig and walks out, following him – the audience cannot see him. HELENA watches them go, and lets THE GIRL out from under tub.)

THE GIRL: How long I stay unda ere like dis?

HELENA: How long? Don't know right now.

THE GIRL: How long you been ere for?

HELENA: Long time. Long, long time. Dey no let me go after de first world war, dey been keeping me for years.

THE GIRL: Since you was how old?

HELENA: Young.

THE GIRL: Ten years, twelve years, fifteen years, whot?

HELENA: Ten – fiftee – ten years.

THE GIRL: And how many years you got now?

(BESSIE enters, goes and wipes between her legs with a cloth, comes and joins them, pulls off her wig and sits back down for HELENA to finish braiding.)

HELENA: Lots of dem.

THE GIRL: Whot? Whot dat mean?

BESSIE: It mean she old! If she knew how many years she had she would have told you a long time ago.

THE GIRL: You no know how many years you got?

HELENA: I neva say dat.

BESSIE: So how many den?

HELENA: Enough to pull your head bald you no shut your mout.

THE GIRL: Do you wanna know? Maybe we can figure it out.

HELENA: No, dat's fine.

THE GIRL: Don't you want to know? I don know, I just tink we should know who we are, whot year we got, where we come from. Dis war not forever.

HELENA: Dat whot it feel like.

THE GIRL: Ya, but it not. I want to keep doing tings. I fifteen years. I know dat. I want to do sometin wit myself, be a doctor or Member of Parliament or sometin.

BESSIE: A whot?

HELENA: So whot has dat got to do wit how many years I got?

THE GIRL: It go hep you to know alla your particulars.

HELENA: Okay – so how you go figure it out?

THE GIRL: Okay. When did dey bring you ere? Which war woz it?

HELENA: It de first one – I say.

THE GIRL: So dat woz 1990 – no?

HELENA: I tink so, I no know.

THE GIRL: I tink it woz. So –

HELENA: No, but it not happen like dat, I was in Nimba County, and Doe men come and dat when I first taken.

THE GIRL: Ya, dat de same time.

HELENA: Oh, okay.

THE GIRL: So how you get to be wit dese rebels when you was attacked by Doe men?

HELENA: Dey find me in de bush when I run.

THE GIRL: And you been wit dem since den?

HELENA: Ya.

THE GIRL: No time you get away from dem?

HELENA: *(Shakes her head.)*

THE GIRL: You remember whot your age when dey catch you?

HELENA: I was small small.

THE GIRL: Before you bleed.

HELENA: Ya.

THE GIRL: So, maybe you had twelve, or thirteen years.

HELENA: Ya.

THE GIRL: So den you now maybe *(Counting on her fingers.)* – twenty-five years.

BESSIE: Whoaw, see, she old.

HELENA: You not so young. How many year she got?

THE GIRL: You no know?

BESSIE: I tink I about nineteen.

THE GIRL: Why?

BESSIE: Because dat when a woman got de juices to have baby and I got baby.

HELENA: She so stupid oh.

THE GIRL: When dey bring you?

BESSIE: I was living in de nort and Taylor men everywhere, den de rebels come and start de fighting – dats when I woz taken. But I tink I been ere since I woz almost a woman.

HELENA: She been ere not too long time.

THE GIRL: You in de nort – I tink dat fighting woz just few years ago.

HELENA: How you know all dese ting?

BESSIE: Ha fada woz in de army.

HELENA: Oh…

THE GIRL: I just know when de army go where – I hear my fada and moda talking and – *(THE GIRL goes quiet, looks away, almost in a trance of silence.)*

BESSIE: So how many years I got?

(THE GIRL doesn't answer, curls up in a corner and looks away.)

BESSIE: Hey, whot ha problem oh?

HELENA: Leave ha. She may be tinking on tings dat happen.

BESSIE: Plenty, plenty happen to me, I neva look like dat.

HELENA: SHUT it, jus go do sometin, go see – he coming.

BESSIE: He no comin, I tek good care of him. I wanted him to sleep so he not go come back again. I mek sure he finish good and thorough. You gon finish my hair?

HELENA: It not easy oh! You got de original African kink! And look at dis comb – it look like it be run ova by truck! You need a new one oh!

BESSIE: When he go back to war I go ask for one – I need new wig, too.

HELENA: You do oh. Dat one more nappy dan your head.

BESSIE: No it not. It still mek me look like Janet Jackson oh.

HELENA: You crazy.

BESSIE: It does, plenty people tell me dat.

HELENA: Like who?

BESSIE: Like CO.

HELENA: CO neva eva say nice ting like dat. He no know how.

BESSIE: He no say nice ting to YOU. He say it to me.

HELENA: Watch your mout oh. You forgetting who Number One. Just because he jumpin on you also –

BESSIE: Plenty, he jumping on me plenty.

HELENA: Dat no mean he like you betta.

BESSIE: Whot it mean?

HELENA: It mean –

(HELENA jumps runs and puts the bath over THE GIRL. The man enters, the women fall in line. HELENA points at herself.)

HELENA: Tought you say you put him to sleep.

(She goes out and glimpses at BESSIE as she does. BESSIE paces, looking agitated. HELENA enters.)

BESSIE: Whot he wont?

HELENA: None a your concern. Startin tomorrow, cook only half of de cassava and save de rest.

BESSIE: Why? Who comin?

HELENA: People comin. Dat all you need to know.

BESSIE: Whot he tell you? *(Sucking her teeth.)* Who comin to eat all our food? We only have small sma –

HELENA: Jus do as I say. Now come I finish your hair.

BESSIE: *(Suddenly in a huff.)* No! I go finish it myself.

HELENA: Dat fine for me! I love to see dat!

(BESSIE sits, attempting to finish her hair, can't balance mirror, can't see what she is doing, tries to comb it, comb flies out of her hand.)

BESSIE: Shit man.

HELENA: You fine?

BESSIE: Leave me.

(THE GIRL knocks on tin bath.)

HELENA: Oh! *(Quickly uncovers her.)* I sorry. You okay? I tink he gone for de night now, you sleep under dere, but we put some stone dere to keep it up so you can breathe.

THE GIRL: Tanks.

HELENA: We gon figure sometin betta for you in de morning.

(*HELENA prepares a bed for THE GIRL and puts her to sleep under tub, prepares herself, and starts to get under covers. BESSIE still struggles with hair.*)

THE GIRL: Tanks.

HELENA: You sure you fine?

BESSIE: I FINE!

HELENA: Good. I gon sleep.

BESSIE: So sleep.

(*HELENA goes to bed while BESSIE keeps trying to comb her hair. BESSIE gasps in frustration, HELENA chuckles quietly.*)

SCENE TWO

BESSIE now asleep with hands still stuck in hair. HELENA is asleep. The tin bath now upturned, THE GIRL is gone. Middle of the night. HELENA wakes up, looks around for THE GIRL, can't find her anywhere. HELENA shakes BESSIE awake.

HELENA: Where de gal?

BESSIE: Hmmm?

HELENA: Wake up or I go trash you! I say where de gal?

BESSIE: I no know, I sleep.

HELENA: Shit, shit, shit, shit.

(*THE GIRL walks in looking dazed.*)

HELENA: Whot wrong wit you?

THE GIRL: (*Doesn't respond.*)

HELENA: Where you go to?

THE GIRL: (*Doesn't respond.*)

HELENA: Whot de matta? I say where you go? Whot did I tell you bout going by you self. You know whot dey gon do to you, dey find you? Do you know? Eh! Speak oh! Who dis gal tink she is eh? You know whot I do to protec you? You betta treat me wit respec, I wife Number One to Commanding Officer General. Dat mean, he trust me de most – I even tell oda men whot to do – if I tell him about you he go –

THE GIRL: He already do it.

HELENA: Whot? Whot you mean? He already do whot?

THE GIRL: *(Numb.)* He already do whot you talking about – he know I ere. *(HELENA is silent, stunned. BESSIE looks on.)*

HELENA: You meet him?

THE GIRL: Ya.

HELENA: He know I keeping you?

THE GIRL: Ya.

HELENA: Where he now?

THE GIRL: He sleep, he told me to come back and go sleep. He catch me when I go to do wet.

HELENA: Whot I tell you about going outta dis compound eh? Whot I tell you. Shit. We gon get it in de morning.

BESSIE: You go get it, I neva say we keep ha from him.

HELENA: Was it jus him? I say was it jus him?

THE GIRL: Ya.

HELENA: You bleed?

THE GIRL: Ya.

(HELENA goes to basin, brings a wet cloth, kneels next to THE GIRL.)

THE GIRL: I wash already.

(HELENA and BESSIE look on at her, shocked, confused.)

HELENA: You okay?

THE GIRL: Jus let me sleep, I say I fine, whot number I is?

HELENA: Whot number whot?

THE GIRL: Whot number wife? He say dere is a rankin.

HELENA: Ah, ah…number four, you number four.

THE GIRL: Whot number is she?

HELENA: Tree.

THE GIRL: So who Number Two?

(HELENA and BESSIE look at each other for a moment.)

HELENA: She no ere right now.

THE GIRL: Hmm…you show me tomorrow whot I do around ere.

HELENA: Ya, I show you.

THE GIRL: Can I sleep ere now? I no have to hide under dat now. *(Indicating tin bath.)*

HELENA: Ya…ere *(Handing her a blanket.)*

(THE GIRL takes the blanket, lies down, and closes her eyes. HELENA and BESSIE watch her in confusion.)

SCENE THREE

Next day, BESSIE is washing soldiers' clothes in a basin and hanging them on the line, HELENA walks in with a bucket of water balanced on her head. She takes it down and pours it into the basin, then joins BESSIE in washing clothes.

BESSIE: I tink she a witch oh.

HELENA: Are you stupid?

BESSIE: She go come in ere talking, 'Hep me oh!' Den she go lay wit de CO, it not even grieve ha! And she askin whot number is she – she act like he not just jump on ha, and she neva know man before! De first time for me I was crying for two days, he not dere, I crying, he come to get me, I cryin, he doin it, I crying, he stop, I crying,

I go sleep, I crying, I was vex. She act like she got no problems. Like notin bad jus happen.

HELENA: Coz she not like you, dat's all.

BESSIE: No, she got sometin off. Maybe she goin off an she not showing it. I go watch ha close close. Whot you tell CO?

HELENA: I say she woz hiding wit de small soldier.

BESSIE: He believe?

HELENA: He no mind, he got ha now. *(BESSIE stops suddenly and gasps as the baby moves, HELENA watches her.)*

You alright?

BESSIE: No, I no alright, I no want it. I gonna hate it.

HELENA: No you not. It gon be nice to have a small one ere.

BESSIE: Are you crazy? It meking me fat oh! You can have it den…why you neva have one, Number One? You been ere for long time. You neva get baby? You can't born?

HELENA: *(She scrubs clothes harder.)* Go check on dat gal, I go finish dis.

BESSIE: Why I go check on ha all de time? She FINE. I tol you she woz go be fine, you worry bout ha too much – when I first come you no –

HELENA: Jus DO AS I SAY!

BESSIE: *(She stops.)* You too harsh man. Fine, I go.

(THE GIRL walks in with firewood, humming a mellow tune to herself. BESSIE and HELENA look on, BESSIE looks over at HELENA for a long moment, goes back to scrubbing clothes.)

BESSIE: *(To THE GIRL.)* You alright?

THE GIRL: Ya.

BESSIE: You fine?

THE GIRL: Ya.

BESSIE: You sure?

THE GIRL: Ya?

HELENA: Shut it, Number Tree.

BESSIE: I checking. Like you tol me.

HELENA: *(Sucks her tongue loudly at BESSIE.)* You know how to make fire? *(THE GIRL nods.)*

HELENA: Good, do dat ova dere.

(She points at fire pit. THE GIRL goes to build fire, HELENA goes with her, watches her closely.)

HELENA: Is you sure you fine? It betta den whot happen to some of de gals out dere, all de soldier get to have dem. Wit us, it just de CO. I know it no feel good right now, but it gon get betta – you gon get use to it – you alright?

THE GIRL: I fine.

(THE GIRL succeeds in lighting fire.)

SCENE FOUR

A week later. THE GIRL and BESSIE are eating.

HELENA comes in with a plate of food. She throws it away, then starts to make a different meal.

BESSIE: Whot? He no want dat? *(Rushing to retrieve the plate.)*

HELENA: He acting like he got a spirit or sometin.

BESSIE: He vex? Whot he saying?

HELENA: He saying de food it taste funny and he tink someone or some spirit trying to kill him. He put a curse on hisself. How God gonna bless a man when he killing moda an chile and stealin and chopping. Den he wonda why he scared of spirits. He want me to make more food and to put dis in it. *(She holds up small pouch.)* He really scare coz o de people comin.

THE GIRL: Whot's dat?

BESSIE: It from de medicine man. It go make so dat no bullet can touch him. *(To HELENA.)* Whot people?

THE GIRL: How it go do dat?

BESSIE: Dat whot medicine can do – don't you know? You no see de rebels dey got de marks on dere arms where dey put de special juju? Dat whot hep dem not get killed when dey fight. *(To HELENA.)* Whot people comin?

HELENA: *(Briskly preparing the meal.)* He gettin more and more mad oh. He actin like bigga devil. And he teking juju, den he keep saying stupid ting like, 'Oh, de monkey Charles Taylor, he got to die, I gon get him'. He don know who Charles Taylor is, whot he done or whot he gon do when he gone. Just talking a lot o notin. But I know why he like dis – he scare cos de women comin – dey gon mek him face hisself.

(HELENA takes food out.)

BESSIE: WHOT?! Whot you mean? Whot she mean? WHOT WOMEN COMING?! Sometin off oh. He tekin his juju and she mekin me cook half de cassava. Sometin off. She no gon tell me dough. I gon watch dem close close. Tink dey can jus be hiding ting from me. I been ere LONG time! I can know all de same ting she know...see whot happen I no doin all de ting I do ere, whot dis place gon be like, I –

(HELENA comes back with several different items in her hands: dresses, shoes, scarves, a radio, a book.)

(Dancing with glee.) Ohhhh, dat whot I like to see, Number One, dat whot I like. I need some new tings, it been too long. Any high heels, some nice wig or sometin, dis one is finished, oh!

HELENA: I gon get de rest. Number Four come hep me. DON'T TOUCH! Keep on doing whot you doin, notin happening ere. *(HELENA and THE GIRL exit.)*

BESSIE: *(Calling after HELENA.)* Don't be sour, oh, I ready for some new tings, just tell me whot I can have and not have. Now dat Number Two gone, I can go second right? Right?

MAIMA: You sound happy I gone, Number Tree, it alright dough, I know you miss me much much.

(MAIMA enters from the other side of the compound, sharply dressed in tight jeans, a slinky top and a bandana, her AK-47 rifle slung snugly over her shoulder. She carries a sack of rice.)

BESSIE: Whot you doin ere?

MAIMA: Where I supposed to be?

BESSIE: Somewhere doing some stupid ting.

MAIMA: I a soldier and dis an army camp, so where else am I supposed to be?

BESSIE: You no solider.

MAIMA: Whot?

BESSIE: I say you no soldier, you a wife like us.

MAIMA: I woz a wife like you. Den I wake up. Ere, I bring special gift. *(Drags in a bag of rice.)*

BESSIE: Is dat RICE! Oh! Dat so good oh we no have rice in long time oh! *(Catching herself.)* But, if you want me to tank you, it not happenin – I know where you get it.

MAIMA: You no worry bout dat, just cook it for us.

BESSIE: You no know how to cook now?

MAIMA: I no cook, dat de job you do. I know you missin me while I out dere, fighting for freedom, so I tought I go pay you visit, let you know I okay, we can have some good food togeda.

(HELENA enters with a few more looted items; she sees MAIMA and is visibly unnerved by MAIMA's presence.)

HELENA: Whot…whot you…whot you wont ere?

MAIMA: Ain't you glad to see me? Stop pretending you no glad to see I alive.

HELENA: I not pretending. Whot I want to know is whot you wont.

MAIMA: See, look how we be treating one anoda! I coming, bringing gifts from war and –

HELENA: *(Getting composed again, but still not able to look at MAIMA.)* We no need no gifts.

MAIMA: You talking like you got a spirit oh! I bringing rice. RICE!!! When woz de last time you see some rice eh?

HELENA: Keep it, we got plenty cassava.

BESSIE: But –

MAIMA: Okay, I tek it to Commando Trigger's wives. I wonted you to have it first – but –

BESSIE: *(Rushing over to HELENA's side.)* Can't we just tek it – she not bad no more, she trying to do good, maybe dis gift from GOD…PLEASE Number One, I so sick o cassava – I so SICK of it – PLEASE, just let ha leave it.

HELENA: *(Ignoring BESSIE, to MAIMA.)* You still ere?

MAIMA: Okay, I takin it. *(Beat.)* You wont to act like you loving on God so much, you neva hear of FORGIVENESS? Dat when you forget de past and give people new chance. You can't do dat, hah? *(She starts to lug rice out, she glimpses over at THE GIRL, who is looking at her intently.)* Who dis?

HELENA: No one.

MAIMA: Dis de new wife eh? You number Four? I Number Two. Where you from?

BESSIE: How you kn –

MAIMA: I know evertin that happens around ere, you don know dat by now? Where you from little gal?

THE GIRL: Kakata.

MAIMA: You likin it ere? Number One treatin you nice nice? She good at dat – in de beginning.

BESSIE: We treatin ha betta dan you would, you have beat ha and shave ha head by now

MAIMA: Stop talking stupid oh, why don't you beat dis rice like a propa little Commandant wife.

HELENA: Don't do notin, Number Tree. Number Two, you ca –

MAIMA: Disgruntled.

HELENA: Whot?

MAIMA: I have a nem of war now and it Disgruntled.

HELENA: I no care bout whot you call yourself – just go. GO!

MAIMA: Oh, so it still like dat eh? You gon kick me out like dog oh? Okay…okay…dat fine, I leave de new family be… for now…but I go come back. *(To THE GIRL.)* Little gal, you let me know you need sometin okay? Number One de Great aint de only one got tings to teach. Dey go tell you, I can do ANYTING.

(MAIMA leaves.)

HELENA: *(Sucks her teeth ferociously as she makes sure MAIMA is gone.)* Tink we gon trow a party for ha or what.

THE GIRL: She got gun.

HELENA: *(Sharply.)* SO?

THE GIRL: *(Cautiously.)* Whot she do?

BESSIE: Mmmm, she bad oh, *(Very quickly, almost manically.)* when I first come, me and ha we use to be good, good friends, she good wit hair oh, and she used to mek my hair nice, nice – dat woz de nicest my hair eva – *(She glances at*

HELENA.) – ah…ah…den she no like dat she not de one CO trust de most – because he be trusting on Number One because dey been togeda long long – den she start to get not nice – she like to fight too often oh, she no like dat he liking me and calling me first when he come from war – den a NEW gal come – dat when it get ugly oh –

HELENA: Number Tree.

BESSIE: Dis new gal woz cute oh. Even I getting jealous small small. And she have dis long hair, I no know how ha hair it growing like dat when she black like me oh! Maybe she a witch – dat whot I tinking now.

HELENA: Number Tree.

BESSIE: Den, I say oh, she go get CO all de time and all de tings he giving me gon go to dis little ting. But Number Two get too jealous oh. Den one day de CO come back from fighting and he got plenty tings. Den he call Number Four. Dat even vex me oh! Number One, she no mind. She no mind noting. Den –

HELENA: NUMBER TREE – shut it oh!

BESSIE: She ask – she ask whot happen.

HELENA: You telling ha plenty oda tings dan whot happen.

BESSIE: Okay – I go say it quick – I go say it quick. Okay, so den – where I woz? Oh, so den – *(Suddenly remembers and laments.)* oh, de rice, Number One, de rice!! Okay, sorry, sorry – so den Number Two see Number Four come back wit alla dese tings and she get new skirt, she get new dress, she get dese sandals, plenty, plenty tings. Den Number Two vex oh – so she wait till we all sleeping den she jump on Number Four – and remember I say Number Four little oh! So Number Two, she beat ha and tek ha tings, she give ha sabou! All dat nice hair she got – GONE – she beat ha face hard oh – in de morning ha face all swollen she looking bad – den when CO call for ha – she scared to tell him it Number Two – cause den Number Two go really finish ha propa, so den she say it a soldier but she no know who cause it dark – den CO tink she loving on anoda soldier so he kick ha out of dis compound. He no like to see his women loving on oda men. So den she go to anoda compound and in de next compound de women are not for one man in particular – dey fo everyone – so now she in bad way oh, all de soldier be having having ha. Den Number One real vex and Number Two and ha, dey be treating each oda bad – so den Number Two she go get into de army to fight – and me I no know how she do dat or WHOT bad ting she doing to people out dere and –

HELENA: You finish?

BESSIE: Ya, I finish oh – she ask.

THE GIRL: She a woman in de army?

HELENA: She devil, dat all…devil. You stay away from ha oh. Okay?

THE GIRL: Okay.

(HELENA sorts all the looted items out and carefully examines each one, folding the clothes with precision after carefully looking them over. Every now and then HELENA looks over her shoulder abruptly and BESSIE backs up.)

BESSIE: You find a good wig?

HELENA: Get back, I say I go sort tru it. *(She picks up a book.)* Don't know whot he want me to do with dis, it a joke or sometin?

BESSIE: *(Taking it.)* I don't know. It a big ting oh, ere, let me tek it, it go keep de fire burning long time.

(THE GIRL jumps up and grabs at it as BESSIE is about to chuck it.)

THE GIRL: I want it! If dat okay.

(BESSIE and HELENA look at her long and hard.)

HELENA: You know how to use it?

THE GIRL: Small small.

BESSIE: Where you learn to use it?

HELENA: Your ma and pa send you to school?

THE GIRL: Ya...my ma...she mek sure I get book learning.

HELENA: When?

THE GIRL: I start five years ago.

HELENA: So you can read and write and do all dem book ting?

THE GIRL: Ya...

BESSIE: Where you go to school? Where you find school in Liberia? She lying, she crazy oh!

HELENA: Shut up ya mout. Dere still are some school left, and she come from near Monrovia, de fighting only been dere small, small time. It about sometin?

THE GIRL: *(Examining the book.)* Ya...

HELENA: Whot it about? Book tings or interesting tings?

THE GIRL: I have to look, de front is tore off...it about a man.

HELENA: Whot man?

THE GIRL: *(Reading.)* Bill Clint – o. Bill Clinto –

BESSIE: Bill Clinto –

HELENA: A white man?

THE GIRL: *(Reading more inside.)* Ya, he white. He from America.

BESSIE: You sho he white? Dere lots of Liberians in America. Maybe he American from Liberia or Liberian from America.

THE GIRL: No, I tink he American from America.

BESSIE: So all dat big ting, it just about dat one man?

THE GIRL: I have to read it first.

BESSIE: How you gon read all dat ting? It go tek up all your eyesight, mek you blind.

HELENA: You stupid. You no go blind from too much book.

BESSIE: How you know? You no read.

HELENA: You no read either!

BESSIE: Number Four, you tell us, can you go blind from book?

THE GIRL: I not sure, but I neva heard of dat.

BESSIE: Dat don't mean it not happen. *(Sucking tongue loudly and goes to her corner.)* Can I have my clothes please!

HELENA: Hold on. Are dose pictures?

THE GIRL: Ya, dere lots o dem.

HELENA: Let's see. *(THE GIRL opens the book and they proceed to look at pictures in the center of it.)* Ya, he white man. He most sure white man. Dis look like it he wife. I wonder if he need anoda.

BESSIE: You want white man now?

HELENA: I no want NO man but how I go survive I don't have one? If I have one I rather have Clinto and not de one I be having now.

BESSIE: How you know he a good husband?

HELENA: You can tell, he good, he go get his wife nice new ting – see how she dressed? Not old ting he steal from civilian. And he gon go places wit her and hold ha hand. He dances wit ha. Dat a good husband.

BESSIE: You want de CO to dance wit you and hold ya hand?

HELENA: *(Sucks her tongue loudly, ignoring her.)* Read some of it to us, Number Four. I want to hear about Clinto.

THE GIRL: *(Reading.)* Oh, look he come to Africa, dis him in Uganda.

HELENA: Oh, he holding African beby.

THE GIRL: He is, it say de beby name Bill Clinto – dey nem it afta him.

HELENA: Eh, Number Tree – you nem you beby afta Clinto maybe he go come rescue you.

BESSIE: *(Sucking her tongue.)* He see me, he gon forget dat white wife. She betta not let him come ere.

HELENA: Read some.

THE GIRL: *(Reading.)* Okay, 'Bill Clinto– in de White Hos. Presid– ' Ah dat word too hard. 'Presi-dental work in de – '

HELENA: Oh, it sounding boring oh.

THE GIRL: WAIT – it gon get good, just give me a few min –

(She stops abruptly, they jump into formation, THE GIRL is called by CO off stage, she slowly and carefully puts the book in a corner and goes out. HELENA goes back to sorting out clothes, she silently puts a couple things aside for THE GIRL next to her book and gestures for BESSIE to look at the rest.)

BESSIE: Wait, wait, wait minute. How you go give ha stuff first before me? I have bigger rankin dan ha! How she gon get when I no look yet? I taking whot I want from dere – *(BESSIE starts to go towards THE GIRL's stuff, HELENA blocks her.)*

HELENA: Eh, eh, eh, don't you dare. Dat MY stuff dat I GIVING to ha. So you IS going second. Tek whot you want. But don't you let me find you taking no ting from Number Four.

(BESSIE backs up, sucking her tongue, she is thoroughly annoyed, goes over to pile and takes all of the items into her corner.)

BESSIE: Dis ting was like it was made for me man! *(Putting on an African print top and matching skirt.)* I look like de first lady.

HELENA: *(Barely looking up.)* Hmmhmm.

(THE GIRL comes back in, walking strangely. She crosses, takes water from near by bucket, grabs cloth, goes to remote corner and cleans under her skirt.)

BESSIE: He quick wit you, he be taking too long with me dese days.

HELENA: Shut yo mout.

BESSIE: Whot? Dat mean he be liking ha more – or she doing sometin dat mek him feel too good. Whot you do, Number Four? I want him to go quick quick wit me too.

HELENA: LEAVE HA!

BESSIE: I no know WHOT your problem is wit dis little gal. She notin special. She your chile or sometin? We all do it, she used to it now. See, look at ha, *(THE GIRL is in her corner, reading her book intently.)* she fine.

SCENE FIVE

Two evenings later. Newly looted radio playing, BESSIE dancing to a few bars of a track.

RADIO: Dat woz de jam number one across West Africa! Miss Economic Community of West African States, Miss ECOWAS happening dis Saturday in Accra, Ghana, where we get to love on our West African beauties. DON'T MISS IT!!! Youssou N'dour and Seun Kuti will be entertaining us all night long!

(Signal starts to fade out.)

BESSIE: Oh, shit man *(She frantically turns the dial.)* Oh, don't stop talking DJ Jay D!!!! Number One, come hep me get signal, it stop workin – it – *(BESSIE stops abruptly, sees MAIMA watching her in a corner. MAIMA is highly amused, with her AK-47 rifle slung around her back.)*

MAIMA: Don stop for me Number Tree, you having disco all for yourself oh!

BESSIE: Whot you doing ere now?

MAIMA: Can't I visit my sistas wit no reason?

BESSIE: *(Agitated.)* Whot you wont?

MAIMA: Eh, eh! You wont to be harsh like dat oh! Fine, ere, I bring special gift for de new gal, *(Holds up a pretty cotton dress.)* she look like she still wearing tings she run tru de bush in.

BESSIE: *(Suspiciously.)* What you want eh? You tryin to do some stupid ting, I know you oh. Leave ha, she don need no dirty dress.

MAIMA: I tryin to tek good care of odas. Dat whot I know to do. Even if you ones don't. You de ones letting ha walk around like she livin wit lizards in de rocks.

BESSIE: You don know how to do notin nice for no one. You betta go before Number One come back.

MAIMA: Oh, ya, where is Number One de great?

BESSIE: She getting wata, she no gon wanna see you.

MAIMA: I no care whot she wont, I my own boss now, I no trying to mek ha happy.

BESSIE: Just go oh, go fight to mek free Liberia or whateva you doin.

MAIMA: Eh, eh, eh, don't talk what too deep for that nice empty head of yours oh. I IS fighting for a free Liberia. If you can carry one tought in dere, carry dat.

BESSIE: LEAVE ME OH!

MAIMA: Eh, why so vex? Fine, here de dress, you mek sure you give ha. If I see it on you, I gon have to tek it back.

(MAIMA exits. BESSIE impatiently watches her leave, grabs dress, looks it over, holds it to her body and places it against herself. She then puts it in her corner and attempts to look occupied just as HELENA and THE GIRL enter. THE GIRL has a bucket of water balanced on her head, HELENA walks in behind her.)

HELENA: Whot your problem oh?

BESSIE: NO! No problem! No problem!

HELENA: *(Staring at her suspiciously.)* We bring wata, Number Tree heat cassava. Number Four, read Clinto.

THE GIRL: Okay... *(Excitedly retrieving the book from her corner.)* so where we woz? Oh...Clinto woz at odds wit de entire government, wit de senate and de house – now both wit Repub – li – can maj – o – ity and seeking his blood if possible.

BESSIE: AHH! Dey gon kill him?

HELENA: NO! Dey can't kill de big man o America!

BESSIE: Dey kill Doe.

HELENA: Dat in Liberia oh! Dat no happen in America!

BESSIE: Dey kill Doe.

HELENA: Dat in Liberia oh! Dat no happen in America!

BESSIE: Liberia and America de same oh! Liberia started by America! My great great grandmo –

THE GIRL: I no tink dey talking bout killin killin. I tink dey talking bout stressing him.

HELENA/BESSIE: Ooooh.

THE GIRL: President Clinto woz still ad – ada – adamant – ly – denying his affair with Monica Lewi – sky, and Congress when –

HELENA: Wait, wait, wait oh. Who is Congress and why he want to catch him and whot is affair wit Monica Lew – is – sky?

THE GIRL: I tink Congress it like government, like ministers, but dey no have to answer to him.

HELENA: Oh, okay – so dey can say whot happen to de big man o de country?

THE GIRL: I tink dey vote and den dey can say yes or no to de big man. But dere anoda one – de, where dey now, *(Leafing through book.)* de Judi – s – a – ry, dey like oda ministers.

HELENA: Why dey need so many?

THE GIRL: I don know. Maybe it to mek sure many people can have say.

BESSIE: So who Monica now?

HELENA: She Number Two, no?

THE GIRL: I tink so – but he not supposed to have a Number Two.

BESSIE: Oh, that like my Pa – he only have my Ma, but den dis witch come and mek him look at ha den –

HELENA: Number Four – can you keep reading.

BESSIE: Oh, wait – why dey want to stress de big man?

HELENA: Oh, ya?

THE GIRL: Dey no like him – dey from anoda group – like he LURD like us and dey wit Charles Taylor men.

BESSIE: Ooooh.

HELENA: Ahh…okay.

THE GIRL: *(Reading.)* It seemed de con – se – kence in mind woz to remove him from his pre – si – den – tal role –

HELENA: Wait –

BESSIE: To whot?

THE GIRL: Dey want to mek him no be big man no more.

HELENA: Why? Because he have a Number Two?

THE GIRL: Ya, den he lie.

BESSIE: Why dat gon mek him not be big man no more?

THE GIRL: I don know.

HELENA: Imagine we have dat ere – dere be no one to rule de country oh!

BESSIE: I tell you, if Clinto see me, he gon want me oh.

THE GIRL: My pa only love on my ma.

HELENA: How you know?

THE GIRL: I KNOW. He good husband. He tell me only be wit man who loving on me.

HELENA: He no know dis war comin when he tell you dat.

BESSIE: Keep reading. I wan de part when he come to Africa.

THE GIRL: *(Suddenly agitated.)* No, I tired now.

HELENA: Tek dis to dem. *(Hands her freshly cooked fufu. THE GIRL exits.)*

BESSIE: She get sour quick oh!

HELENA: She missing family, dat all. *(THE GIRL returns.)*

THE GIRL: He say he wan to see you. *(HELENA exits.)*

BESSIE: You miss your pa and your ma?

THE GIRL: Ya… *(Tears brimming.)* I wan my ma.

BESSIE: I tink mine dead. But I tink I go find my broda when it ova. *(HELENA re-enters, with a few new loot items.)*

BESSIE: NO!! He get more? When dey go fight?

HELENA: Dey been gone two days.

BESSIE: Oh. I no realize. Whot he bring?

HELENA: Tek, I don want anyting.

BESSIE: TANK YOU! *(She grabs things from HELENA, sorts through them ravenously.)* Oh, dis is NICE! Oh, I no like dat, whot is DIS! He crazy oh, he tink we grandmodas, ere Number Four.

(THE GIRL takes pile, a packet of hair extensions fall to the floor.)

BESSIE: Oh, I wont dat! I no see dat!

HELENA: Eyy, you let ha have it so now it hers.

BESSIE: She no want dat anyway!

THE GIRL: I wouldn't mind –

HELENA: Ah, den it hers Number Tree, you already have your hair done anyway.

BESSIE: NO! I need it – I higher rankin dan ha!

HELENA: Ya and you give it to ha so now it ha's.

BESSIE: I no agree.

HELENA: So whot? I Number One and I say –

BESSIE: If she de big man of dis compound den whot are we?

THE GIRL: Whot are we whot?

BESSIE: We de ministers, no?

THE GIRL: Oh, we de Sen-ate and de Judiciary.

BESSIE: So I as de Sen-ate – say 'no' to de big man.

THE GIRL: Okay, den I as de Judiciary, I say 'yes'.

HELENA: So whot I say go – de extensions are for Number Four.

BESSIE: Shit man. *(Goes to her corner, scowling at THE GIRL and HELENA.)*

HELENA: Come I braid it for you Number Four.

THE GIRL: Oh…okay

(THE GIRL goes to sit down; when called by CO, points at herself and goes. BESSIE sulks in corner, HELENA leans back and closes her eyes, BESSIE starts to inch toward HELENA, watching her as she does, she gets close to extensions, and attempts to take them.)

HELENA: Don't even.

(BESSIE, retreats, deflated.)

BESSIE: It no fair, I NEED those, I having baby and I gon get bigger and ugly, I need my hair to look nice at LEAST.

HELENA: You not gon get ugly.

BESSIE: Yes I is, you know how des women look when dey have beby, dey face go big like it got air and dey eyes go small like bird and dey lips go wide like dis and dey look BAD. I want to use de hair to cova my face small, small.

HELENA: You gon be fine. De CO not gonna jump on you so much.

BESSIE: I know, dat de one ting. He gon be on Number Four PLENTY, coz he no jump on you no more and – ah… ah…whot I say? I no mean to say like dat whot I –

HELENA: Just go sleep.

BESSIE: Okay. *(She goes and lies on her mat.)* You tink Clinto's Number One angry wit him?

HELENA: Ya.

BESSIE: You tink dey all living togeda nice nice now – like us?

HELENA: I no know – I no tink dey do it like us.
I tink de women can leave.

BESSIE: Number Two leave…

HELENA: She no leave, she just fightin wit dem now. Dat not de leaving I mean.

BESSIE: Ya. Dat true.

HELENA: Number Tree?

BESSIE: Ya?

HELENA: You been savin de cassava like I tell you?

BESSIE: YA! Tell me whot happening. What you keeping keeping de cassava for?

HELENA: I gon cook it all in de morning.

BESSIE: WHO COMIN?

HELENA: Neva matta. No one you gon find interstin. Number Tree?

BESSIE: Ya?

HELENA: Sleep.

BESSIE: Fine.

(THE GIRL enters, goes and wipes between her legs, and curls up on the mat. HELENA blows out torch.)

SCENE SIX

Next day. At camp, by the compound, RITA, a member of Liberian Women's Initiative, an upper-class, well educated woman; throughout she occasionally speaks 'Liberian English' like the women in the camp but her proper English often takes over. She is relatively new to the struggle for peace and functions awkwardly in this rough terrain. She approaches HELENA, who is pounding cassava with a mortar and pestal.

RITA: How tings?

HELENA: *(Surprised.)* How tings? How you come follow me out ere? I got to finish dis *(Indicates cassava.)* You need sometin?

RITA: No, ah…I just…I…I wanted to see how things going out here.

HELENA: Whot?

RITA: And to tank you for de cooking it was very good so tank you.

HELENA: You off oh?

RITA: Whot you mean?

HELENA: How you go tank me for cookin? Dat whot I do, dat whot we do ere, how you tank for dat, you off oh.

RITA: That not all you can do – dere much more you could do – no one should expect that from you. *(Beat.)* I know I am not really meant to be out here *(Looks around cautiously.)* My colleagues like to follow some rigid protocol when we meet with the COs. But I believe we should take every opportunity to meet you gals. Rita –

(Rita looks around the compound, intrigued, horrified. She has obviously never been in a place like this before.)

HELENA: Well, you betta go. *(Beat.)* How you come here? How it okay for you to come here? Why he let you in, treat you good, give you our cassava, not mek you a wife like us?

(Beat.)

RITA: Okay. *(Beat.)* Well, we are a part of a large network of women peace makers, it is our mission to end dis war. Right now we are negotiating with the factions to immediately obey the ceasefire, to put down their guns. The only way to do that is to come to these different warlords and talk them down.

(Beat.) They have been doing this for a long time, they – ah – *we* have quite a reputation in de country now, it allows *us* to come and go like how you see.

HELENA: Why he so scare of you?

RITA: He isn't scared of us.

HELENA: He is! He told no one do notin to de Peace women when dey come, he no treat no one else like dat. And he been using his juju a lot just now.

Dat how I know he scare de most, when he using dat stuff. It mek his spirit go quiet. So ya, he scare of you.

RITA: Well good. GOOD. They scare of us, maybe we can actually get them to the point where things change and they stop acting like BEASTS, trying to treat us like we village girls they rob from de bush.

HELENA: *(Coldly.)* Is dat right.

(An awkward pause ensues for a few beats.)

HELENA: Why you do all dat stuff?

RITA: Why? Why you tink? You happy with Liberia as it going? You tink dis a nice place? Look at de tings going on my dear! Look at where YOU are! You tink it normal you wifing some dirty self-proclaimed general in de bush? You tink it normal a boy carrying a gun killing and raping? You think it okay dere no more schools, no more NOTIN! I had to WALK my son from Kakata to the Ivory Coast just so he could stay in school!

HELENA: Okay, you don have to get vex.

RITA: Sorry…I…

(A few beats pass, HELENA stores ground cassavas, RITA starts to look around curiously.)

RITA: So…do ah…any other gals comin around lately?

HELENA: *(Suspiciously.)* Why you asking me dat?

RITA: If I…if I could get you out of ere – would you go – would you go with me?

HELENA: Go where?

RITA: You can go to school, you can –

HELENA: Where I gon go to school

RITA: I can get you in a camp in Cote D'Ivoire or –

HELENA: Where dat?

RITA: Ivory Coast

HELENA: Oh. So why you calling it sometin else?

RITA: No mind. Why would you not go?

HELENA: I don know.

RITA: Would it be a hard choice? If I could get him to agree, would it be so hard to leave this?

HELENA: No...but...

RITA: You happy ere?

HELENA: No, but dis is war and I whot else I gon do?

RITA: You know all the things you can do if you go to school, the ways you can improve your life! You can get your own business, own your own house, take care of your children –

HELENA: I no have children.

RITA: But you might have them! Things could be over soon, you have to think about whot your life can be.

HELENA: I no know, I wife Number One I been wit him for long, long time. I tek care o him, I –

RITA: The war ends – are you still wife Number One?

HELENA: I...I no know who I is out of war – dat not whot I get to tink about.

RITA: I am going to hep you – it is going to end.

HELENA: I got tings to do ere, tings no gon happen propa I go. I tek care o CO. I have rank ere now. I can tell de small small boys whot to do. I care for de oda women. And dere lots o tings we doin ere now – we even reading book in de compound.

RITA: Whot book?

HELENA: It about de big man of America, Clinto.

RITA: Clinton?

HELENA: Ya. And his government. And Monica his Number Two and how de Judiciary and Senate and Starr trying to stress him. *(RITA laughs.)* We no know if he stop being big man because of his Number Two or not – we no get dat far yet. You know whot happen? If you know don't tell me notin.

RITA: I no gon tell you. But you know that happen long time ago oh. Five years or so.

HELENA: We no mind, it still good story, don tell me whot happen. *(Beat.)* But, you know, when I look at you, you know all dese book tings – I do wan to learn – I neva go to school – I do want dat. It just…I just don know if I can learn now – I getting old to be sometin different.

(HELENA walks out, taking the cassava with her. RITA watches her for a bit, thinking. She grabs a stick, and starts to write in the dust. HELENA reenters.)

HELENA: Whot you doin?

RITA: Writing my name. Whot's yours?

(HELENA stares at RITA for a long beat.)

HELENA: My nem? Numba One

RITA: The one your ma and pa give you!

HELENA: NO. I wife Numba One to the Commanding Officer of LURD Army – I –

RITA: WHAT DID YOUR MOTHER CALL YOU?

HELENA: I – I neva use it – I –

RITA: You MUST know it. Tell it to me – now.

HELENA: It…it…I can't

RITA: *(Seeing HELENA is shaken.)* Okay, it's okay, just whisper it to me, try. *(RITA holds HELENA close, putting her ear to her.)* Come on gal. *(HELENA whispers something inaudible into RITA's ear.)* That's beautiful! Here let me show you whot that look like – *(RITA writes HELENA's name in the dirt.)* There – you do it – *(Hesitantly, HELENA takes the stick and writes out the same letters.)* Good…good…very good *(HELENA finishes writing her name.)* That your name. You just do it.

HELENA: No lie?

RITA: No lie.

HELENA: It not that hard!

RITA: No, it not! Now let me show you what each letter it is –

HELENA: I can't believe OH! I do book ting! *(RITA laughs.)* I gon tell de new gal! *(RITA stops dead, stands up.)*

RITA: Whot? Whot new gal?

(Lights.)

SCENE SEVEN

THE GIRL enters, humming a tune, she picks firewood and places it in a wheelbarrow. After a moment she picks up a stick, starts writing something in the dirt with it, MAIMA enters, unseen by THE GIRL, she watches her for a beat and then:

MAIMA: So you city girl eh?

THE GIRL: *(Startled.)* Yah.

MAIMA: I know Kakata well well. I get supplies from dere all de time. You run for long time?

THE GIRL: *(Cautiously.)* Some…some days.

MAIMA: Ya, dat hard eh. But you look strong oh. Like you got a lotta powa!

THE GIRL: Powa?

MAIMA: Ya. I can see your eyes, dey got fire! And your arms and legs – dey strong oh.

THE GIRL: *(Giggling, embarrassed.)* No!

MAIMA: Yes! You got to tap dat powa oh. You tink God give all dat to you for notin? You tink God let you survive for notin? You got to do de tings you called to do oh. Is dis it? Picking firewood in de bush? Dis whot your powa for?

THE GIRL: I…I don know. *(Giggles again.)*

MAIMA: Whot? Whot so funny oh?

THE GIRL: It just…it just…Number One say you devil, but you talking like you prophet.

MAIMA: Number One say dat eh?

THE GIRL: Hmmhmm! *(She continues to giggle. MAIMA laughs too, though in a different tone.)*

MAIMA: Ya…ya dat funny oh. *(Beat.)* How you like *Numba One*?

THE GIRL: She fine.

MAIMA: *(Lighting a cigarette.)* She kick me out oh. Ya…Some stupid gal was lovin on anoda soldier who beat ha. Den she gone tell Numba One dat it my fault she get trown out – Numba One believe ha and not me – She crazy oh.

THE GIRL: What about de sabou?

MAIMA: HA! So dey tell you already. Dey not gon tell you how dey getting all dose tings de CO bring from war eh? How he getting dem *(Taking a long drag on her cigarette. Then vexed.)* He giving WORSE den a sabou! HA! But dey wann act like dey clean o all sin or sometin. You trust who you want. Like Tupac say, Only God can judge me. *(Putting out her cigarette.)*

THE GIRL: So where you get dis den? *(Tugging on jeans.)*

MAIMA: Kakata.

THE GIRL: And dis. *(Indicating earrings.)*

MAIMA: Dis…dis from de big city.

THE GIRL: You get tings from de big city!

MAIMA: Ya. *(Laughs.)* Plenty tings. Didn't you like de dress?

THE GIRL: Whot dress?

MAIMA: What? Dat STUPID gal. I go fuck ha up good. *(She sucks her teeth.)* I brin you dress. So you can look betta dan dis. So you can look good like me. Don worry, let ha have it. Whot you wont? Tell me whot you like.

THE GIRL: Nail varnish.

MAIMA: Ah, which color – you look like you like de red one, or de purple.

THE GIRL: Pink.

MAIMA: *(Laughing.)* Okay. Dat good! You have to decide whot you wont. Dis is war, how you gon survive? Dis is how *(Indicating gun.)* – den you can prospa – you can get every color of de rainbow nail varnish, it no matter whot happening. And most important – no man gon touch you. *(Examines her closely.)* So de CO he like you, ha? He jump on you a lot? You like dat? Look at me. Is dat whot you want? Hmmmhmm? Did you like dat?

THE GIRL: No.

MAIMA: *(Militarily.)* Whot?

THE GIRL: NO.

MAIMA: So whot you gon do? Let me tell you de last time a man jump on me. In fact, I can't remember, all I know is he not know I have gun. He dead now. No one gon jump me again. Now, I choose who I lovin on. Because of dis. Whotever you wan, it's yours. Just go get gun.

THE GIRL: I can't…no…

MAIMA: It easy right now – dey need soldier – dey so desperate for fighter now, dey tek baboon if dey could teach it who to fire. Ere, *(Hands her gun.)* try it – hold it.

THE GIRL: I don –

MAIMA: TRY.

THE GIRL: *(Takes gun.)* It heavy oh.

MAIMA: Now hold it like dis and you point it forward – Now fire.

THE GIRL: No, I scare.

MAIMA: Scare of whot? FIRE! GIRL FIRE!!

(THE GIRL fires the gun. She gasps, panting. Adrenaline flooding her system. MAIMA, pleased, affectionately strokes her head.)

SCENE EIGHT

At camp. Next day. HELENA is cooking and intermittedly changing the channels on the temperamental radio. THE GIRL is painting her nails. BESSIE is leaning against a crate, eyes shut, breathing hard.

BESSIE: *(To HELENA as HELENA changes radio channels.)*
Wait – dat good song – WAIT – Dat music oh!
Whot your problem? Let de songs play oh!

HELENA: I not looking for music.

BESSIE: Whot you want den?

HELENA: Neva matta. *(Beat.)* I want to know whot happenin.

BESSIE: Where? What happen in wit whot?

HELENA: Wit de WAR.

BESSIE: You got a spirit dat too strong oh. So you want to hear dose people just talkin and talkin?

HELENA: Yes. It called *news.*

BESSIE: Who –

HELENA: SHHHH your mout oh!

RADIO: ...as fighting intensifies approximately one hundred women all dressed in white marched to the U.S. Embassy in Monrovia calling for immediate and direct intervention by the U.S. government leading to… *(Radio crackles and dies.)*

HELENA: *(Sucks her teeth.)*

BESSIE: And we coulda be listening to music all dat time oh! *(Changing position with discomfort.)* Was dat one a de peace women I saw you talking to?

HELENA: Ya.

BESSIE: Like de ones who come last time?

HELENA: Ya.

BESSIE: Dat who woz comin?

HELENA: Ya.

BESSIE: Oh dat borin oh. Why she talking to you? I tought dey not talking to us, just to de CO. I tink dey witch oh, dey can talk to CO like dey men or someting.

HELENA: Dey not witch.

BESSIE: Whot? So why dey can do dat? Dey got some strong juju. Dey off oh.

HELENA: No. Dey been workin on dis stuff for long time from de city so de CO have to show dem respec dat all.

BESSIE: Ya coz dey witch.

HELENA: Not everyone witch!

BESSIE: *(She adjusts her position with difficulty.)* Ahhh…senate want to pass bill. It de – 'No work when baby coming' bill. I can't do notin – I hate dis, I HATE DIS!! I no feel good Number One.

HELENA: Stop talking like you a small chile, you go HAVE a chile, act like it oh!

BESSIE: I shoul neva listen to you, I no want dis ting.

HELENA: You go have it, and you go love it, cause dat whot a moda do.

BESSIE: I no want to BE no moda. You say you go tek care of it. You betta. An you KNOW you go tek care of it if it got a face like dat ugly fada of it. Read Clinto Number Four.

THE GIRL: I no tink he too ugly.

(HELENA and BESSIE stop and stare at THE GIRL curiously.)

THE GIRL: He got a big nose, dat is true, but he no too ugly, his eyes and his mout not too bad.

BESSIE: Dere sometin wrong wit you. Really someting wrong oh.

HELENA: And where you get dat from? *(She indicates the nail varnish.)*

THE GIRL: Whot?

HELENA: DON 'whot', whot you tink? Dat ting you holding in your hand.

THE GIRL: Oh…dis wos gif.

BESSIE: Gif from who?

HELENA: EEEEY! You no ask ha notin! I wife Number One ere ha? So shut ya mout. A gif from who?

THE GIRL: Dey tol me not to tell.

HELENA: TOLD YOU WHOT? I no tink you understand where you are. You are in my territory, little gal, I am de 'Commanda In Chief' in dis ere country of dis compound – EVERYONE do like dey is tol, dey follow command. You don wanna see wha –

THE GIRL: Dat not whot she tol me.

HELENA: Whot?

BESSIE: Whot she say?

HELENA: Whot you say?

47

THE GIRL: I SAY…dat not whot she tol me.

HELENA: Who? Who tell you WHOT?

THE GIRL: She tell me dat she woz de one de CO love de most even dough you wife Number One /

HELENA: / Oh, of COURSE –

THE GIRL: / DEN, den, she watch how you always mek it so everyting go tru you, jus like when de loot come de oda day and you de one who decide who get evertin firs and you decide who get whot /

HELENA: / HA!

THE GIRL: / AND she say she bring me nicer tings dan whot you get and Number Tree steal whot she bring me and –

BESSIE: *(Hastily.)* She a LIAR oh! She lyin Number One, I tell you true –

HELENA: She back again? WHERE she be?

THE GIRL: She go again, wit de soldier, she go to fight.

HELENA: Where you see ha?

THE GIRL: Out dere when I go to get de firewood.

HELENA: So whot? You like ha? You wanna fight now eh? You wanna be in de army?

THE GIRL: I tinkin about it.

HELENA: She tinkin about it.

BESSIE: Tinking!

HELENA: You no know notin little gal! NOTIN. You tink you can fight, you go do dat, you go see whot happen to you – de ting you go end up doin out dere. You wanna kill a man, a woman, a small small chile? You wanna do dat, hey?

THE GIRL: No, but I no gon do dat.

HELENA: How you no gon do dat? You go do whot da commanda tell you go do. If he tell you go kill dat village and bring him tree wives, you go have to do dat.

THE GIRL: She no say dat, she say –

HELENA: She go say good ting coz she wan you to be like ha, but she LYING to you.

THE GIRL: No, she tell me she get whotever she wont from de civilian, she tell me she only go for Charles Taylor men, not de modas and de children.

BESSIE: Let ha go! She crazy oh!

HELENA: SHUT YA MOUT! You no know whot you talking about little gal. Dey go mek you do all de ting you see when you and you family have to run, all dose ting and worse. Do you know whot she do? Whot dese soldier do? Whot dey done in my presence? Dey gon mek you slit a moda's stomach and tek out de beby to see if it boy or a gal.

Dey gon mek you –

THE GIRL: *(Explosively.)* I NO GON DO NO TING LIKE DAT!!! But if I soldier, I no have to stay ere no more!

HELENA: It betta ere den –

THE GIRL: NO it not. Look at ha! She gon have his beby! I NO WANT DAT!!

HELENA: We can stop dat, dere is dis leaf you can chew –

THE GIRL: I NO WANNA CHEW NO LEAF! I want him to leave me alone. I just want to get AWAY FROM HIM! Now she gettin big, he gon jump on me all de time, he no want you no more, and I no want dat! If I got a gun, don nobody gonna fuck wit me no more. I wan dat.

HELENA: Dat whot she say? No one fuck wit ha now?

THE GIRL: Ya, dat whot she say. And dat whot I wan.
(She gets up, walks out.)

ACT TWO

SCENE ONE

Two days later. The middle of a shootout. MAIMA fires some shots in the direction of random gunfire. They crouch close to the ground. THE GIRL holds her gun close to her body and stares on. She attempts to prep her gun and it gets stuck and she falls, struggling to unjam it.

MAIMA: Okay, listen good oh! Check de ammo for any dents in cartridges. Now, when you put de magazine into dat hole dere – put dat forward lip of de magazine into de hole first. Ya. And be sure de magazine it flat down. *(THE GIRL dislodges magazine and does as instructed.)* Good. Now you pull de charging handle to de back, all de way…all de way and release. You have to know how to do dat quick quick.

THE GIRL: Okay.

MAIMA: Now come *(THE GIRL hesitates, starring at the carnage in front of her in distress.)* COME.

(THE GIRL cautiously approaches her.)

MAIMA: You see dat one dere?

THE GIRL: Ya.

MAIMA: Dat de enemy – now fire him.

THE GIRL: Why?

MAIMA: Whot?!

THE GIRL: Why we firing dem? Why…why dey choppin de men like dat? Why can't we just let dem go somewhere, run away, why –

MAIMA: I don't know whot you talking about. To me, dat is de ENEMY. Do you know dey harboring lots of Charles Taylor men ere? Do you know whot dey could do to you? Dose are de monkeys who kill our mas and rape our grandmodas.

THE GIRL: But dey just living ere – dey –

MAIMA: EEEEYYYY! *(Grabs her face and looks deeply in her face.)* LISTEN TO ME! Dose are Charles Taylor's monkeys! Dat who we fightin. We are fighting de monkey Charles Taylor. He eating and drinking and living like a king in a land of paupers. We drive him out. And we gon keep on putting on de pressure. He scare of us. We gon do him worse dan dey do Former President Samuel K. Doe. We gon catch him and dress him like a woman before we kill him. We gon restore Liberia to its rightful people. You understand, de enemy, de enemy is no longer human being. Okay?

THE GIRL: Okay.

MAIMA: *(Redirecting their attention to the fighting.)* Now…see dat one?

THE GIRL: Ya.

MAIMA: Fire him. Do like I show you, NOW.

(After much hesitation she shoots with her eyes closed.)

MAIMA: Ah, come on – *(Holds gun in direction of man.)* Fire again. FIRE.

(THE GIRL shoots.)

MAIMA: Good gal. Now you doin sometin, you hepin us get closa to freedom. One monkey at a time. You don't go nowhere. Stay down okay? *(MAIMA gets up and goes. Moments later MAIMA returns.)*

Okay, it's ova. You do good. You do good, good. Round up de young gals.

THE GIRL: Whot young gals?

MAIMA: You'll see dem as you walk around. Round dem up. Dat's your job.

THE GIRL: Where we gon tek dem?

MAIMA: Back to de camp.

THE GIRL: For whot?

(MAIMA doesn't respond.)

THE GIRL: Whot? For de generals? *(MAIMA doesn't respond.)*

THE GIRL: NO, no no no no no. How can we do dat to dem
– den de same ting dat –

MAIMA: You want it to be you? You want to do it in dere
place? Dey won't mind, dey will tek anyting. Dey is
beasts and beasts need to be fed. It dat simple. We have to
provide dem wit fresh meat or dey go find it some oda way
and you don't want to be dat oda way, do you?

THE GIRL: But I thot you say dat –

MAIMA: You feed dem, you not get eaten. Dat simple. Go and
get de gals or I go have to tell dem you want to replace de
gals today. Is it you or dem? Dis is how you survive, you
understan? So is it you or dem, Number Four?

THE GIRL: Don't call me dat.

MAIMA: Den go get de gals. If you want a name of war, act
like a soldier and HUNT. Go. Go on gal. Go. GO.

(They stare at each other for a long moment and THE GIRL goes.)

SCENE TWO

*One month later. MAIMA leads RITA to a makeshift latrine in the army
camp, MAIMA's gun firmly clutched. RITA wears a T-shirt with the words,
'DIALOGUE DIALOGUE DIALOGUE' across the front.*

MAIMA: So right now I looking to find some sound system.
It right ere. *(Pointing at latrine with rifle.)* You know dose
in high demand, oh.

RITA: Is dat right? *(Trying to mask a grimace as she examines
latrine, positions herself, and squats to urinate.)*

MAIMA: Ya! See, you women from de city you tink
we backward out ere, we know whot is happenin,
we got radio, Bose, evertin out ere.

RITA: Ohhh!

MAIMA: *(Runs to RITA, pulling rifle into position.)* Whot matta?

RITA: Notin. I just almost fall in.

MAIMA: Don't do dat, you gon get a shit bath you fall in dat!
I sure you used to betta, you women from de city, but dis
all we have ere.

RITA: Dat fine, dat fine. *(Adjusting her clothes, coming out from
latrine area.)* Thank you.

MAIMA: So. You got some tings to sell from de city?
Some rice, some cloth, tings like dat? We can mek our trade
on a regular. You come and bring tings from de city den I
gon sell it out ere in de bush. One a my men he heping me
sell. We can do good business. You got some tings?

RITA: No, noting.

MAIMA: Noting? You say you was businesswoman.

RITA: I was. I woz in big business, big, big business. Not whot
you tinkin. *(Almost reminiscent, almost with pride.)* I had a
petrol station, two supermarkets, a hair salon – you know
dat woman at all the important events with de big, big
head wrap and a lot of makeup? Dat woz me. *(Beat.)*
I doing different work now.

MAIMA: Whot? Dis peace ting? Dat not gon bring you no
profit oh! You woz doing good oh! We could have work
togeda! It best to work wit de system, and right now –
de system it war.

RITA: De war gon end, it gon end soon –

MAIMA: How you know? De fightin getting stronga! LURD is
getting bigga! We tekin more an more!

RITA: I know, people are dying, for no reason. De fighting getting closa and closa to Monrovia. It real bad now. We was just ere a mont ago and we had to come back again. Your CO got to stop dis. He got to tell his army to stop.

MAIMA: Stop for WHOT?! Dis whot we got to do to get rid of de monkey Charles T –

RITA: Charles Taylor not de only problem. We see de villages you LURD be tekin ova, modas, grandmodas and children dying. Dat got to end too, don't you tink? Aren't you tired? Don't you want to go home to your family? To move forward? Where you from?

MAIMA: I from Liberia.

RITA: Whot is your name, the one your family give you?

MAIMA: See, I know whot you women try to do. You trying to mek us weak. You want us to start to feel like little gals crying – 'Ooh, I lost my ma, ooh, ooh, I lost my pa, dey hurt me, dey rape me'. I no do dat no more, go to de villages if you looking for stupid gal like dat. I hep mek women strong. Dat whot I do. You want cryin little ladies, go to de Commandant wives. Me, I no care about –

RITA: Do you miss your ma? What did she wont for you when you get big?

MAIMA: EH, EH! Who you tink you talking to? YOU, you women, you come up in ere like you – *(Gaining her stride.)* We all know de REAL reason you doin dis – no man wont you so you got notin else to do but botha us – you need a man? Let me try see I can find you one. It may be hard! You not so fresh no more

RITA: *(Aghast.)* You rude little ting. *(Explosively.)* You who runnin around witout a tought in your head, showing off wit dat stick dat kill people. And trading your pussy for profit –

MAIMA: *(Agitated.)* EH EH EH! WHO YOU TINK YOU TALKING TO? You know de tings I go do to you, you not protected by de Commanda?

RITA: *(Regaining her composure.)* Okay, okay, okay…I apologize for whot I just said. I do. I do. *(Beat.)* I ask you about your moda, about your name because you don't wont to lose dat, you must neva lose dat. *(She reaches out to touch MAIMA, MAIMA backs up violently.)* When I lose ha…those LURD boys just tek ha. Dey knock me down with their guns and drag ha away. I busy shouting, 'Do you KNOW WHO I AM!' Dey didn't care who I woz. I woz just another woman to be abused. And she had tings, tings she wanted to do, to be, she wanted to be a businesswoman like me or something. And it MY fault because I know that I could have protected her better than that. I should have gone to Ivory Coast or Ghana or something. I stayed ere because I wont to profit from war, tinkin somehow my money gon keep me safe. It didn't do noting for me dat day. How long you tink you can mock God before He mock you back?

MAIMA: Who you talkin about? *(Beat.)*

RITA: My…my daughter…I talking bout my daughter. So please, please trust, I ere to hep – I suffering too.

MAIMA: LURD tek ha?

RITA: Yes.

MAIMA: Ha. So dat why you ere. Actin like you ere for peace talks. Dat why you coming out all de time, talking wit us even though de oda women you wit stay at de CO compound. Actin like you care bout us – you just lookin for your daughta ere. HA! Well, I not ha, so you can get offa me oh.

RITA: No you not ha. You certainly not. *(Beat.)* But I am also ere to hep.

MAIMA: Hmmmhmmm!

RITA: I am! And I looking at you right now. And I wont to know – who is your moda and whot is your nem; I gon give you shit until you see whot you doin is gon kill you and your heart gon cut and God gon mock you back and –

MAIMA: God not gon mock me! He heping me, coz I hep myself. So don't you worry about me. Go look for your daughta and leave us be oh. *(MAIMA starts to walk out, turns back.)* Ha, how I gon learn from you oh? Whot you teach your daughta not hep ha. If she had learn wit me, wit dis, *(Indicating rifle.)* maybe she still be around

(MAIMA mockingly gestures 'After you' with rifle. RITA after some hesitation starts out, with MAIMA following behind.)

SCENE THREE

The next day. Army Camp, THE GIRL, rifle in hand, dressed sharp in a tight pair of pants and matching shirt, new hairstyle.

THE GIRL: 'Firm your jaw! FIRM YOUR JAW! You can't be tinking about mama and deddy anymore! Listen to me – I am now you moda, your fada, your grandmother, your great grandfather, your ancestors, your Creator, your Jesus and your Allah. You belong to me. You will be listening to me all de time. You will do whot I say, when I say do. Touch your nose – I say touch your nose – good. Good. Stand up! Sit down! Stand up again! Good. Now, there will be no crying, no galie talk and no period cramping ere. I am your Superior! You will be doing what I say when I say do!' *(To MAIMA.)* Den I say some gon be wife and some soldier.

MAIMA: *(Emerging from behind her.)* Dat good! Dat good oh! You get betta about it!

THE GIRL: …Ah…ya, it getting betta wit de gals. I just remember whot you tell me –

MAIMA: *(Pleased.)* Whot? Whot I say?

THE GIRL: Dat dis is war, and you can't tink too much and God keeping my conscience for me – it gon be clean and new when dis ova.

MAIMA: Dat good oh!

THE GIRL: Tanks!

MAIMA: So where you workin?

THE GIRL: De check point, wit Rambo.

MAIMA: Whot you do?

THE GIRL: *(Excitedly.)* Oh ya! I just tell dem – you can't tek dat big bag a rice all dat way! Den I say, just leave it here, I'll tek care of it. When I see woman wit nice cloth, I just tek whot I like from ha, den I say, 'Proceed tru de check point, proceed!' Look, I get some Timberlands – dey a bit small, but I stretching dem out. Dey just do whot I say do! Den dis one man – I fire him. He had too much money – we jokin – we call him Charles Taylor's son! But we scare he got too many connection so I had to fire him.

MAIMA: Whot you got for me?

THE GIRL: *(THE GIRL hands her half of a wad of money.)* And I save you sometin. Look at dis. *(Hands her a shirt she took off a civilian.)*

MAIMA: I no like dat.

THE GIRL: Oh, sorry.

MAIMA: But dis is good oh, you acting like solider afta a short time oh! How long you been wit me?

THE GIRL: Ah…about a mont.

MAIMA: See! You doing real good job oh! I woz worrying about you, now I see everytin fine oh!

THE GIRL: Ya, I okay. *(Beat.)*

MAIMA: You lovin on someone?

THE GIRL: Huh?

MAIMA: I say you lovin on someone?

THE GIRL: NO.

MAIMA: You want to?

THE GIRL: *(Bewildered.)* I...I don know.

MAIMA: You need to be lovin on someone – it go hep you be
   protected. You chose someone you like, high rankin –
   den I hook it up.

THE GIRL: I tought you say if I have gun –

MAIMA: You have to have someone – it hep. Den you can start
   your business like me. Right now, I lovin on tree men. If I
   not lovin on no man I not gon have de tings I want. I just
   gotta mek sure I wit a man of high ranking. And one of
   dem he got high ranking. De oda one, he got good business
   but de third one, he de one I like, he de one got my heart.
   (She giggles like a girl in love.) De one wit high rankin, he got
   many women, but I his favorite dough. He give me de most
   tings when he come home from war. But whot I really want,
   whot I looking for right now is a four wheel drive, one a my
   men teach me how to drive so now I go buy and sell and go
   back and forth to Monrovia. You need one. We will find you
   one. Okay.

THE GIRL: Ya...okay.

SCENE FOUR

*Two weeks later. RITA and HELENA at camp, in compound. The
compound looks markedly more sparse, with the cooking station
manifesting clear signs of neglect. HELENA fiddles with the radio which
now has an elaborate makeshift antenna attached to it.*

RADIO: ...the LURD rebels are now closing in on Monrovia,
   having taken over eighty percent of Lib – *(Unintelligible.)*
   ...intensive fighting for the past six weeks since early
   June... *(Unintelligible.)* ...displaced citizens in the sports

stadium… *(Unintelligible.)* …while the peace talks in Accra are at a deadlock the… *(Unintelligible crackle ensues, HELENA finally turns it off.)*

RITA: Da fightin so bad I don't even know how we going to get back. How de CO actin?

HELENA: He actin mad oh. He say dey tekin Monrovia den dey gon live in Charles Taylor's hos. Dey talking about Charles Taylor hos an we no got notin ere. Lots a dem in my unit gon and not coming back.

RITA: You seen dat gal yet?

HELENA: No, but my small soldier been wit ha. He saying she still close, say she looting civilian plenty. She getting de gals for de commandas too, she –

RITA: My God. AHHHH! Who she wit?

HELENA: Number Two – she calling haself sometin foolish now like Misgruntle or sometin.

RITA: Disgrunted?

HELENA: Ya.

RITA: Dat Number two?

HELENA: Ya, you meet ha?

RITA: Ya…I meet ha. *(Under her breath.)* Oh my God.

HELENA: She devil, she do bad tings. But Number Four not like ha. Number Four she…she special gal…she read to us – she tell us tings she wont to do – she –

RITA: You find out where she from?

HELENA: Ahh…she say Kakata.

RITA: Ha.

HELENA: She say ha fada woz in de army dere – but she talk about ha ma de most, ha ma –

RITA: And she got book learning?

HELENA: Ya. *(Beat.)* Who knows where dey be now?
I been praying for Number Four.

RITA: *(Turning away.)* Hmm, okay.

HELENA: Whot…you no pray?

RITA: Ahh…no…no I don't. And these women I am working
with, they…they prayer warriors oh. I'm not into all dat.
I'm not…good…

HELENA: *(Delicately.)* Okay, you wanna to try?

RITA: *(Very hesitantly.)* Ah…not…not really…ah…

HELENA: It not gon do you notin harm oh. It mek me feel
betta. I see you got sometin heavy on you – praying it mek
tings not so heavy.

RITA: *(Stares at HELENA for a long moment. Finally.)* Okay…
okay, you…you go ahead.

HELENA: Okay. *(HELENA kneels and takes RITA's hand.)* God,
bring Number Four back, protec ha, keep ha safe in body
and mind, convic her heart to come back to sense, show
ha your love *(Beat.)* and I pray for Mama Peace, Lord, that
she might know ha work it not in vain. We pray in Jesus
His love precious Amen.

RITA: *(Beat.)* Amen. *(Beat.)* Thank you.

HELENA: Tank you.

*(BESSIE walks in, heavily pregnant, with a new but shaggy wig that
covers most of her face.)*

RITA: I have to go – oh…hello!

BESSIE: *(To RITA.)* Oh, good, you ere again! You bring
cassava?

HELENA: Number Tree –

RITA: No…ah….no I don't have anything actually.

BESSIE: NOTIN! We no got no food oh! Why you come ere and you no hep –

HELENA: NUMBER TREE!

RITA: You have no food? Noting?

BESSIE: NOTIN!

HELENA: *(To BESSIE.)* EEEYYYY!! *(To RITA.)* He…he gon bring some…we'll have sometin soon.

RITA: Goodness…

BESSIE: Well you can read us book at leas! I missin Clinto!

RITA: Ah…ah…of course, of course…oh my goodness how are you – you haven't been eating – *(Indicating BESSIE's belly.)*

BESSIE: *(Handing book to her.)* Oh dat. *(Indicating belly as though it isn't attached to her body.)* Dat fine! De olda woman from de next compound is midwife. Read, just small small.

RITA: Okay… *(Opening book.)* Just a little. Do you know where you were?

(BESSIE and HELENA look at her blankly.)

Whot woz the last thing you remember hearing?

HELENA: Oh, he woz to go to court, den he get to not go.

RITA: Okay, *(Leafing through book.)* let's see.

BESSIE: You tink we send him letta, he gon get it?

RITA: You want to send Bill Clinton a letter?

BESSIE: Ya. I just wont to tell him I glad he still de big man and I like his story.

HELENA: She mad oh! She tink de big man of America gon read letta from us.

BESSIE: Why he not? America our fada – we founded by Americans – so he our big man too.

RITA: That is true but…uhhh…about that – I should tell you something…

HELENA: About whot?

RITA: About Clinton being the big man…

BESSIE: Oh, ohh, oh oh.

HELENA: Whot your problem oh?

BESSIE: I do wet – but I no do wet.

RITA: Oh my goodness. Where de midwife? We tek ha?

HELENA: Ya, she not far, grab ha arm.

(They help BESSIE up, her wig falls to the ground as they escort her out.)

BESSIE: My wig, oh, get my wig!!! I need it to cova my face small small! De wig oh!

SCENE FIVE

A week later. THE GIRL rushes in and falls to her knees, weeping and attempting to pray.

THE GIRL: Our fada – Who are in – sometin…hollow your nem, de kingdom dat be yours…de kingdom dat be yours come – on eart and in…sometin, for de powa…you de powa…

(MAIMA enters.)

MAIMA: You do good work. So you get your nem today.

THE GIRL: *(Wiping tears away quickly and sitting up.)* Whot dat?

MAIMA: De nem dat mek you a soldier.

THE GIRL: Okay.

MAIMA: Ya, so tell me, why are you fightin?

THE GIRL: *(Reciting what she has been taught.)* We are fighting for de liberty of de people.

MAIMA: And who are we fighting?

THE GIRL: We are fighting de monkey Charles Taylor. He eating and drinking and living like a king in a land of paupers. We drive him out. Once he gon, we stop. And we gon...and we gon...

MAIMA: ...keep...

THE GIRL: We gon keep on putting on de pressure...
we gon keep on putting on de pressure...

MAIMA: He scare of us. He neva gon come out and fight like a man. He wont to hide behind all his security. We gon strip him of all a dat. We gon do him worse dan dey do Former President Samuel K Doe.

THE GIRL: / Former Samuel K. Doe

MAIMA: We gon catch him and dress him like a woman before we kill him.

THE GIRL: Sorry.

MAIMA: Jus keep learning it. If any of de Commanders come to you dey go be vex you don know dose tings. So why is you fighting? Choose sometin you want to fight for.

THE GIRL: My moda.

MAIMA: Why?

THE GIRL: I...she just who I want to fight for.

MAIMA: Whot you want for her?

THE GIRL: I want ha to be happy, to be blessed by God.

MAIMA: You gon fight for your ma? You go see justice served so you ma and all de mas of Liberia blessed and not in pain no more?

THE GIRL: Ya.

MAIMA: Den dat your nem.

THE GIRL: Whot?

MAIMA: Moda's Blessing. *(Beat.)*

THE GIRL: *(Searching.)* I tink…I tink I cursed.

MAIMA: Whot? You tink you whot?

THE GIRL: I CURSED. She curse me, she say, she say 'Devil bless you', and now I, I, I can't remember whot my moda she look like! I can't remember! I go, I go get de gals like I always do afta fighting, but dis one, she looking all nice in ha nice cloth, she acting like she betta dan me, I wanted ha to shut ha mout, to show me respec. She kept saying, 'Devil bless you!' Now she keep coming back to say dat to me, in my head, she won't shut up her mouth! Den I say okay, I can fight this ting, I just remember my moda saying 'God bless you' – and dis thing gonna disappear. Den, den, I can't see my moda no more! I can't hear my moda no more! I just hear dis gal! *(Beat.)* I had just wanted to shut ha up. I tought…I tought…It neva happen like dat before, I got system. De men have to come to me and discuss which gal dey want, I give dem one. I tell dem – dis gal special, she your wife, she only go wit you. But wit dis one – I didn't protec ha like I usually do – I just let dem tek ha, because she woz talking too much. *(Beat.)* Dey do it right in front of us at de camp, dey don't care, dey don't care dat God right dere, dat He can see whot dey do. Dey just keep jumpin and jumpin on ha, it five o dem and I see she too small, she just little, small small den me. I want to say stop but I scare dey gon come to me if I say sometin. *(Beat.)* I see she stressed, she start to vomit – it look like rice or oats or sometin, den ha eyes start goin back. I can't move; den, den ha eyes just go still, she starring right up to de sky and she not moving; de fifth one he just keep going till he done. *(Beat.)* She got blood everywhere, dey leave ha lying dere and tell one o de small soldier to go get wata so dey can wash deyselves, dey tell me and anoda small soldier to trow ha in de riva, I just do like dey say, I too scare to say noting. I tek ha arms and he tek ha legs, she still bleedin and bleedin, ha eyes still looking up, I no look at ha no more. We drop ha in de riva and I pray, I pray dat God bless ha soul, dat He no blame me for whot dose men do. But it my fault she dead, and she tell me 'Devil bless you', and now I can't even see my moda no more! I cursed. I got dis sin on me and I gon go to de devil straight.

MAIMA: EYYYY!!! FIRM YOUR JAW. *(Slapping her.)* I say FIRM YOUR JAW! I say firm your jaw, FIRM IT. *(Hitting her and beating her continuously, passionately.)* Don't you eva, *(Beating her.)* EVA *(Beating her more.)* come to me wit dose STUPID stories – you understan? You got to be STRONG! Dis is war little gal. And you a soldier. *(She stops beating her but holds THE GIRL's jaw firmly in her hand.)* Whot does a soldier do in war? SPEAK!

THE GIRL: Dey fight.

MAIMA: Ya, dey fight. We winning, we even stronga and stronga now. So you betta fight little gal. You Moda's Blessing now, you SOLDIER, you understan?

THE GIRL: I understan.

(MAIMA releases THE GIRL abruptly and roughly escorts her out.)

SCENE SIX

Same evening. BESSIE at camp, with an infant strapped to her back, she sings to herself, as she coos at her baby, and sweeps the compound – THE GIRL enters and stands silently in the corner, her face obscured by the dark. BESSIE finally sweeps at THE GIRL's feet.

BESSIE: *(Startled.)* FUCK SATAN, HEP JESUS! Number Four! How you gon come on me like dat?

THE GIRL: I sorry.

BESSIE: Whot you doing ere, Number Four? I not see you for long time. I thought you Commander General by now!

THE GIRL: Moda's Blessing.

BESSIE: Huh?

THE GIRL: My nem, it...it Moda's Blessing.

BESSIE: Okaaaay. So whot you wont?

THE GIRL: You getting beby?

BESSIE: Hmmhmm.

THE GIRL: Oh, he sweet oh!

BESSIE: It a gal.

THE GIRL: Oh, ya, oh I see ha betta now, she look like you. She pretty.

BESSIE: Tanks. I like ha. I did not tink I woz go like ha, but I do. She no look like him, she a small small me! How I no gon love ha? I look at ha, and she look at me wit dose eyes and all dat stuff coming out ha mout after she drink milk and I say, If any body do sometin to my chile, ever – dat de only ting dat gon mek me pick up de gun and fire you, den I curse you, curse you to de devil. Dat when I gon go to de medicine man for true and get some o de juju dat go hurt someone, dey go wake up with no privates or sometin. Dey go fire dey self – dey be so vex. *(Beat.)* I neva felt a love like dat, you know. I kill and curse for ha. And I tink God will be on my side. I sure of dat. How you? You should get beby, it feel good.

THE GIRL: No, I can...I don wont dat. Where Number One?

BESSIE: She wit de CO.

THE GIRL: I go wait for ha. Ere, I bring gif.

(She pulls out a large cassava root.)

BESSIE: That so good oh, cassava! It been too long oh! *(BESSIE grabs the cassava root and rushes to cooking station. She searches for a knife to peel and chop the root.)*

THE GIRL: *(Looking around.)* Whot dis? *(She picks up a tattered piece of paper.)*

BESSIE: Oh, dat dis ting Number One keep doin – she learn to write sometin, she keep writing it ova and ova – she going mad oh! Guess whot we learn about Clinto? He not de big man no more! It a Bush. A bush! Dat his name – a Bush! Like in de bush – you know?

THE GIRL: Ya, I understan.

BESSIE: Dat funny oh!

THE GIRL: Ya. Where Number One?

BESSIE: I tol you she wit de CO. Whot vexing you?

THE GIRL: Notin.

BESSIE: Okay. *(Goes back to peeling.)*

(RITA rushes in, excited, looks around for HELENA.)

RITA: Where's Number One?

BESSIE: SHE WIT DE CO! Whot wrong wit you people oh!

RITA: I have to tell you all something. *(Notices THE GIRL.)* Oh…

BESSIE: She Number Four.

THE GIRL: *(Automatically.)* Moda's Blessing.

RITA: Oh…oh God…oh God… *(RITA, trembling and fighting tears, advances towards THE GIRL.)* It not ha…it…it not ha…it not. *(Shaking her head and looking to BESSIE in mournful agony.)*

BESSIE: Whot you talking oh?

RITA: Ah…ah…ahhhh…ah…noting. Noting. *(Collecting herself for several beats. To THE GIRL.)* Rita Endee, I am a member of the Liberian Women Initiative for Peace –

THE GIRL: Oh.

RITA: So…so whot is your name?

THE GIRL: I tol you – I –

RITA: Whot is your real name – the name your mother and father gave you?

THE GIRL: *(Struck.)* Oh…

(HELENA enters, a dazed look on her face, she looks over the compound, not even taking RITA and THE GIRL in. Methodically, almost robotically, she starts to pick up things and pack them up.)

BESSIE: Whot you doing?

HELENA: Hmm?

BESSIE: Whot you packing for, Number One?

HELENA: Helena. H-E-L-E-N-A. Helena. Dat my nem. I not sure about my last nem, I tink it Sowa, Sona, or sometin. I tink it Sowa. I need to remember all dese ting now. Where I from? Buchanan? Whot I go do now? Whot I go do now? *(Starts laughing.)*

BESSIE: You go mad oh?

HELENA: *(She finally takes in the room.)* He call me over, he say sit down. All de years I be wit him, he neva have me sit down. Maybe sit on him, but neva he sit me down to talk to me like human to human. Den he say, 'De war ova, Charles Taylor go to Nigeria, you can go. Pack your tings and go. We going home.' Den he get up and walk away. Dat it. All dose years, he tek all dose years, he mek me leave my chile when we running from Taylor men, he, he mek my chile die in de bush, all alone – he mek it so I no get born no more, he mek me so sick my stomach broken, den he go just trow me away like dat. I cook every meal he eat, I know all de secret of his unit, everyting, but he just go spit me out like dat, like I someone he just meet yesterday. *(Starts to laugh.)* I scared oh! He say, 'you can go'! I can just go, wherever I want – de war it ova! Do I have ma? Do I have pa? I no know, 'You can go', I don know whot GO means! Whot it mean? I tink, I tink I gon go to Monrovia, sell tings, get a business, but I wont to go to school, I wont to learn to do sometin, to read like you Number Four – you can be member of Parliament now! Did you hear? We can all GO! Let's GO, Ma Peace! I can go now! You free, Number Four – you no have to fight no more. Don't do no bad tings no more – dat not you, gal, dat not how God mek you. He mek you good gal.

(HELENA hands THE GIRL her book. THE GIRL slaps HELENA hard, grabs her rifle and points it at HELENA's throat, pushing her back until the rifle is touching HELENA's throat. She releases almost primal sounds of aggression, her eyes flashing something verging on demonic. She stands there, seeming to will herself to drop the gun and pull the trigger simultaneously. RITA stands petrified, then seems to will herself to advance towards THE GIRL, and speak to her softly.)

RITA: Gal…gal…listen to me. I am a member of Liberian Women for PEACE. I gon hep you gal, I gon hep you – You don't wan to do this. Dis is not you, dis not whot God make you for.

THE GIRL: Whot he mek me for?

RITA: Good tings, he mek you for so many good tings. Look at her, she wants to read now – why? Because of you, because of you my daughter.

(THE GIRL looks over at RITA, searching, THE GIRL breaks down, drops her rifle and drops to her knees and weeps. RITA removes rifle, drops to her knees also and gently strokes her back, THE GIRL crumples into RITA's arms. RITA clings to her with yearning compassion. Silence ensues for several beats. BESSIE's baby starts to cry.)

RITA: *(Stroking THE GIRL's back, to BESSIE.)* How is she?

BESSIE: She fine.

RITA: She's just a few days old huh?

BESSIE: She young, young.

RITA: Whot's her name?

BESSIE: Clintine.

RITA: Oh, Clementine – that's Fre –

BESSIE: NO! Clintine.

RITA: Clintine?

BESSIE: Ya.

RITA: Okay, that, that's lovely. We need to move. The Commander General is letting you go – these camps are dismantling so I can get you all some help. There is a truck we are catching – about fifteen minutes from ere. We rounding up as many of you women as we can, but there is no time! We have to go now. There is still some fighting so we have to get to the main road really carefully. But the major crisis is over, Taylor is gone! So I am going to take you gals to a camp – further north, near Guinea –

BESSIE: I tink I go stay.

HELENA: Whot you say?

BESSIE: I go stay wit CO.

HELENA: Stay to do whot?

BESSIE: He de fada of my chile, he de only man I know to be wit for long time. Whot I go do out dere? I can't learn to do tings, dat not me.

HELENA: So you go follow CO around wherever he go?

BESSIE: Ya, I go home wit him. He like lovin on me, he no gon mind. *(MAIMA rushes in.)*

MAIMA: Moda's Blessing, so you run ere like beby eh? Let's go.

RITA: Where are you trying to take her?

MAIMA: Dat not your problem – she soldier.

RITA: Taylor is gone.

MAIMA: I know dat. Dat don mean it ova. His monkey soldiers still everywhere. Whot dey tink? Dey tink we go just stop now?

RITA: You got to stop, it ova! The ECOWAS forces are killing any rebels still fighting. They are going to have disarmament and you have to turn in your weapons –

MAIMA: Dey can turn in dey modas! I not letting my gun go for notin. Moda's Blessing – LET'S GO!

BESSIE: Leave ha! She gonna stay wit Ma Peace and Helena.

MAIMA: Wit who?

HELENA: Wit me. It ova oh. Just stop, you should just stop it while you can.

MAIMA: Shut your mout. Stop for whot? Den whot? No way. And since when you care about whot happen to me eh?

HELENA: I always care about you. Dat why I can stand to see de tings you doing. But you can stop now, it ova.

MAIMA: *(Stares at HELENA for a long beat. Finally.)* FUCK YOU! Moda's Blessing –

HELENA: Leave ha, Maima.

MAIMA: Whot you call me?

HELENA: I call you your name.

RITA: De war ova, get back to who you woz. You go back out there fighting, you not gonna make it.

MAIMA: You God? NO! So you no know notin about whot gon happen to me. YOU NO KNOW. DIS WHOT I KNOW TO DO. *(Breaking.)* WHAT YOU TINK EH? WHAT YOU TINK? YOU TINK I GONNA BE LIKE MY MODA begging at de refugee camps, pleadin around for a cup a rice den dey just jump ha till she dead when dey supposed to be protecting ha? Tink I gon let dem treat me like I is notin! NO WAY! DAT NOT MY STYLE, DAT NEVA GON BE ME! *(Desperately.)* MODA'S BLESSING COME ON! COME WIT ME! LET'S GO! You gon stay? *(Beat.)* You stay, you gon wish you come. You stay, you no gon have NOTIN. You just go back to being weak little gal. *(She leaves sucking her teeth.)*

(Silence for a few beats as they watch MAIMA go, RITA shaking her head.)

RITA: *(To THE GIRL.)* You gon be okay. You can find your family now.

THE GIRL: I don't tink I have any, my pa dead and my moda, dey, dey tek ha and den dey –

(THE GIRL stares at BESSIE – her face immobile. The women all stare back at her in a prolonged silence, absorbing all that isn't said in full understanding. Finally.)

RITA: We have to go.

HELENA: Okay –

BESSIE: Okay. Bye.

HELENA: Bye. Stay wit God eh, don't stay wit CO forever – he gone waste you.

BESSIE: I be fine.

RITA: Whot is your name, my daughter? The one your mother and father gave you?

BESSIE: Oh, dat? It…it Bessie.

RITA: Good, okay Bessie, I cannot just leave you – please, come, you can –

BESSIE: I be fine. I be fine. I WAN stay. Dat whot I wont.

RITA: Okay… *(RITA gives up. To HELENA and THE GIRL.)* Come, we have got to go now. Here, let me help you. *(She helps HELENA gather up her things.)*

(RITA and HELENA exit. THE GIRL goes and grabs her book, stumbles on her gun, stops, picks it up and looks at it and looks after where MAIMA exited. She stands there with book and gun in hand behind BESSIE who sits on the floor with her daughter, cooing her and singing to her gently. THE GIRL doesn't move, seemingly transfixed to the floor, unable to walk in either direction. Random gunshots can be heard in the distance. As BESSIE sings, the lights fade out.)

BESSIE: Clintine, Clintine, you so pretty like mama
– Clintine, Clintine!

END OF PLAY.

DANAI GURIRA is an award-winning Zimbabwean American actor and playwright. As a playwright, her works include *In the Continuum* (Obie Award, Outer Critics Circle Award, Helen Hayes Award), *Eclipsed* (NAACP Award, Helen Hayes Award for Best New Play), *The Convert* (six Ovation Awards, Los Angeles Outer Critics Circle Award) and *Familiar*, which had its world premiere at Yale Repertory Theatre in February 2015. All her works explore the subjective African voice. She is the recipient of the Whiting Writers' Award, is a former Hodder Fellow, and has been commissioned by Yale Repertory Theatre, Center Theatre Group, Playwrights Horizons and the Royal Court Theatre. She is currently developing a pilot for HBO. As an actor, she has appeared in the films *The Visitor, Mother of George, 3 Backyards* and the television show *Treme*, among others. She currently plays Michonne on AMC's *The Walking Dead*. She is the co-founder of Almasi Collaborative Arts, which works to give access and opportunity to the African dramatic artist. Danai was born in the U.S. and raised in Zimbabwe by Zimbabwean parents. She holds an MFA from NYU's Tisch School of the Arts.